SAY SOMETHING

By

JEREMY CLARKE

BASED ON A TRUE STORY

Introduction

Have you ever been ask

"Are you okay."

And you freeze

Taking a breath

Swallowing

Every pain

Every hurt

Every scream

That wants to come up

And you respond with a smile

"Am great, and you."

Who taught us how to lie?

This is my story

This is about the person you see every day

The person in the crowd

The person in the mirror

This is the story of when you hurt and do not heal

Say Something

Contents

ELIJAH

Home

The early 1800's

On a ship called

The Creole

Sailing from

Virginia to New Orleans

To sell the slaves onboard

135 enslaved Africans

After ten days at sea

19 of those slaves

Overpowered the guards

And took control of the ship

With plans to sail to Liberia

But with limited supplies

They came to Nassau

Nassau, Bahamas

Settling in Gambier

A settlement established by

Sir James Carmichael Smyth

GAMBIER

I am the last child

Between my mother and father

Fourth inline

They lived in a village

Gambier

She was in love

And he was abusive

The village felt like a box

Or maybe a nest

I always felt

If I jumped to high

I would hit my head

On the ceiling of expectations

But I loved it

It was by the sea

Sometimes we blindly

Justify bad things

I remember the church

My Grandmother went too

It sat on a hill

Facing the sea

A reminder

That God is everywhere

A church

That now holds

The body of my mother's parents

Who I miss every day

PRISCILLA

My Grandmother

It was always my belief

That my Grandmother

Was the dream

God had for Eve

God gave me

13 years with her

13 years of showing me

What an angel could me

What a mother could be

And love like the air

That we often take for granted

She was so strong

She worked at a clinic

And odd jobs to provide for her family

When people think of home

They think of a place

When I think of home

I think of my Grandmother

Her heart a fireplace

Shelter from the wilderness

It is true what they say

That people may forget

What you did

But they will never forget

How you made them feel

WILLIAM

For my entire existence

My Grandfather has been blind

The house we call home

He built himself

Long before losing his sight

I am proud

To be his descendant

Of such a strong man

I get my will to be

From him

Although he was blind

He did everything for himself

He was so strong-willed

Every time he cleaned

He would say

"This house has more sand than the bay."

He never complained or made excuses

He simply thrived

Despite it all

MOTHER

Like a diamond

Carve from coal

You gave life to me

Like the sun alone

In the open sky

I was yours

I thank you

For being there

It is easy to look back

To reflect

To see the cuts

That became scars

I used to lay awake at night

Worried about you

Still at work

Getting off at midnight

The darkness

Hides so many things

GROUND ZERO

My father abused my mother

Am too young to remember

I have no memories

Of the first four years of my life

No pictures as proof of my existence

I was a single friend

On a married couples retreat

Everyone is too busy to notice

My mother

Too young

Overwhelmed

She had three kids

In three years

All in the same month

Exactly one year apart

Then three years later

She had me

ZONE ONE

1994

First Semester of

Grade 1

Gambier Primary

School on the hill

Seconds from home

I raise my hand

To get the teacher attention

"Can I use the bathroom, please."

No

Was the response

I sat there

And I peed in my chair

Was sent home to change

I remember my mother

Dressing me again

Sometimes the demons we face today

We created many moons ago

Be careful with power

FAMILY

As a child

I was always observing

Like I was watching T.V.

Family always seems

So odd to me

Distant

But so near

It felt like

I spent my life

Living with roommates

So numb

I feel nothing

No magnetic pull of love

Just silence

Imagine a tree growing

With all its roots

Above ground

Without the comfort of

Mother Earth

But it grows

None the less

Adapting to life

I was given

It is this reality

That made me realize

That anyone can be family

Love cannot be forced

It must simply be

PAIN THAT NEVER HEALS

Birds

After being in the nest

For so long

Are forced out

So that they can

Spread their wings

And fly

I never got a chance

To enjoy the nest

The nest is filled with thorns

That made resting uncomfortable

There was always something wrong

The pain never healed

Old wounds ripped open again

And I just keep swallowing

Pushing the pain away

To the dark

Empty

Spaces of my mind

Until

Here I Am

Numb

Like a wild horse

Locked away

I just seek freedom

I was too young

To know what pain was

Too young to have it

But I did

It surrounded me like water

Like this island, I live on

I never screamed

I never ask for help

From a child

I could see

Everyone around

Was in pain

How could they help?

When they are

Still trying to help themself

CHRISTMAS

I remember

Christmas day

Standing in the kitchen

With all my emotions

Bottled up

For it was Christmas

The day of Jesus birth

As I try to comfort myself

As I tried to be happy

But am staring out the window

As if locked away

Seeking freedom

I look out

Seeing the road

Every child in the village

Has new bikes

I could have cried

But as always

I kept it together

I was forgotten again

That story

If your good all year

Santa would give you a present at Christmas

Was just a story

I was forgotten

I stood in the kitchen

And the mask cracked

But it was not broken

It was not the lack of gift

That bothered me

It was the feeling of emptiness

The feeling of being abandoned

No one remembered me

It hurts

But I push it

In the dark spaces of my mind

I put on my mask

And I continued to pretend

MAMA'S BOY

I have a few memories

Of my father

The word Father

Leaves a bitter taste

In my mouth

Another pain

That has not healed

I have a few memories

Of my Father

Like a few days

Out of the years

I have been alive

Writing this

Ignites a flame in my soul

Awaking old empty memories

My father made a choice

That as his child

I was not worthy

Of his time and love

He abandoned me

Forgotten again

I mourn for the child

That never was

As a child

My father was alive and well

He had used my mother

Until she had enough

He looked for a new victim

My father's like to be taken care of

A mama's boy

Like my older brother

His Jr

My brother

Became my father

To my mother

I WAS NEVER ENOUGH

One day

Sunny and calm

I went to the kitchen

Took my older brother

And my only brother

Tennis racket

I was alone and bored

I went to the nearby tennis court

By myself

And I just hit tennis balls

To pass the time

I remember coming back

My mother and brother were home

He was angry

That I had taken his racket

That is my family

I said in my head sarcastically

My mother

Thought that I deserve

A slap to the face

So, she did

As she slapped me

I hit my head

Into the corner of the back door

I ran into the couch

In a flood of tears

Holding my head

I open my eyes

Everything was blurry

Because of the tears

I looked into my hand

And there was blood

There was blood

Coming out of my head

Over a tennis racket

That is the level of love

That existed in this house

In this family

So, my mother had no choice

Took me to the hospital

She said to tell the doctor

I was hit my rock

And I did not know who threw it

So, I lied

Got some stitches and left

I say this

Not to make my mother appear cruel

Because between my mother and father

My mother won by default

I say this

So that one can understand the damage

A parent can do

That can last a lifetime

POOR BUT SMART

September 1999

The first day of Grade 6

My mother was unable

To buy me a school bag or books

I told my teacher

Before class began

Her name was Mrs. Clarke

Same last name as mines

After hearing my story

She decided to give a speech

At the beginning of class

About how she did not care

And it was not her problem

If we did not have books or a bag

I felt shamed

I felt the sting of poverty

There was nowhere to hide

I was shocked

That a teacher could be so cruel

But like so much pain before it

I endured

Never told anyone about it

June 2000

The end of

Grade 6

I finished 1st in that class

I was always resilient

I remember being home

In our one-room apartment

Way to small

But it worked

We were all in the living room

This is where

The mask I wore

Harden

My mother

Had only a dollar to her name

Sent me to the store for a biscuit

I had never seen

Such happiness and sadness all at once

Poverty is humbling

But it can create

A spirit

Of gratefulness

HIDING

As a child

I wanted my family happy

I thought that was normal

But it was not

It was unhealthy

I thought if I neglected myself

And focus on their needs

Everyone would be happy

Like Jesus on the cross

I thought if I sacrifice myself

I could make their world better

Thoughts of a child

There was no one there

To correct me

No one there to say

Live your life

Enjoy the beauty of childhood

Instead

I was a caterpillar

Turned into a butterfly

Trapped in a jar

For everyone amusement

Except for my own

And the mask hardens

The mask is what I pretend to be

Happy with fake smiles

Afraid to speak

Afraid to have a problem

Afraid to ask the adults

To raise me

Instead of watching me

INFECTION

Have you ever been

Surrounded by people

But so alone

Like the last tree

In a once beautiful forest

Hope and sadness

Intertwined

I hear sounds

But I hear nothing

I see you

But who are you?

I feel nothing

So numb

I do not know

How feelings feel

Like I do not belong

But my soul on fire

To fight this darkness

But my heart

My heart build walls

Evolution?

Adaptation?

I cannot give you

What I do not have

So, I give you this mask

Maybe you will love

The me

I pretend to me

Who do I turn to?

Except

Myself

Accept Me?

IS IT TO LATE?

BEND

It is hard to describe the pain

That is always there

Pain that you have become so used to

They say bend

But do not break

But even if you never break

You are never the same

It is easy to look back now

And think differently

Like a rat in a maze

That has found the cheese

You have not won

Just been distracted

As a teenager child

I took it all in

And never let it out

Time passed

And the tree bended

And here I am

Teenager

Airplanes

Gambier was near the airport

The planes would be so close

They would shake the whole house

Small aircraft and huge planes

I loved them all

I used to go outside

And watch them

And wonder

Where they were going

Or where they just came from

They made freedom seem possible

I used to wish

They would take me away

I felt stuck

Like my wings were broken

All I wanted to do was fly

There were no movies

To tell you how to cope with pain

I was not home alone

Just alone at home

At 13

My Grandmother died

I still remember it

Surround by her children and husband at home

I walked past her door

She was dress in white

Her last minutes on earth

Cancer had claimed another victim

The next time I would see her

Would be at her funeral

At 13

I was not allowed in the room

I went to the backyard

With my cousin Paige

Then the silence was broken

By the loud cries of my uncle

And I knew she was gone

I did not want to feel

I know that sounds weird

But I was so numb

Emotions require effort

I did not want to feel any more pain

My Grandmother

Was the glue that keeps the family together

The most beautiful soul

I ever saw

Was her

And now she was gone

All the broken pieces

That I call family

Would become unloose

I felt the most for my Grandfather

The women he loved

And the mother of his children

Had just died

To add to that pain

He was blind

I can only imagine his feeling

Not being able to see her one last time

That is a pain

I hope never to feel

LEFT AGAIN

My father

Was hardly in my life

Father a word

Am trying to become accustomed to saying

I knew his face though

The face

That found me unworthy of his love

But I had my mother

Until now

16

Left Again

At 16

My mother moved overseas

I was never sat down and told

I just knew about it

She needed a break

A break from her family

That cut a hole so deep

No words can describe

At first, I was happy for her

Which child does not want their mother happy?

Even though I never call her mother or mom

In her absence

It soaked in

My mother needed a break from me

Abandoned

Still in school

Not sure who was suppose

To take care of me

Probably no one I guess

The mask became like skin now

In between

My two older sisters' apartment

And grandparents house

I was parentless

And my mind reminded me

That intelligence has its drawbacks

LOST

Like a bus

That is full

And passes you by

That feeling in the pit of your stomach

Of being left

Of what could have been

Missed opportunities

OUTSIDE IN THE DARK

Late at night

After Midnight

I was asleep in my sister's bed

With my nephew

Her son

He was about two years old

My sister was out

Having a good

As she usually is

Her boyfriend

My nephew's father

Came to the window and knocked

I told him

She was not home

A few hours later

My sister came home

Furious

That I had told him

She was not home

She was enraged

Like waking up, the neighbors enraged

My mind could not comprehend it

And she belittled me

I will not repeat her words

But I had enough

It was perhaps this night

That I began to find the power of words

She then physically put me out of the house

As our older sister looks on

I sat on the porch

In the dark

And I cried

For the first time in my life

I was tired

I kept saying

I am tired

I am tired

I was tired of it all

It was too much

My mind could not take any more

How can you be so kind to people

And they treat you so horrible in return

I wanted to walk to the police station

But it was too dark

I was afraid

So, I just sat there

And cried

Eventually

She let me back in the house

Saying she was sorry

But it was too late

Family had betrayed me

TRYING

Am trying

Like the moon at night

Am trying

But no one likes the darkness

Even when we sleep, we dream

Searching in the darkness

My tears like rivers

Carving mountains in my mind

Am trying

But am tired

Of having to be

Everything

Hot and cold

And am cracking

WHY AM I HERE?

Home in the village

Staring out the window

There was a tree

That is still there

It produces no fruit

But long leaves

Long colorful leaves

That said

Here I Am

It always reminded me

Of Joseph and his coat of many colors

It was different

Like me

But am staring out the window

Sitting down

In loneliness

Pain and emptiness

A question came from within

Why am I here?

I felt no warmth

No love

No purpose

Staring out the window

Asking questions

Not of myself

But of the world

Of God

It was this day

That I found God

I cannot describe it

I looked out the window

And from within

I asked

Why am I here?

I never really talked to God

I prayed for health and strength

And assume HE knew my problems

Of course, he did

But I never ask for help

FREINDS

I had such amazing friends

Lawrence

Javier

Durante

Akeem

They offer an escape

From the reality of home

Many days

We stayed at school

Until it was dark

Until the only thing

We saw on the road

Were the bright headlights of cars and buses

No one expected me home

I probably could of stay out forever

We made sure

Each other was okay

The library was our home

So many laughs

So many memories

Each one of us was unique

But so similar

It was these friends

That made me appreciate

The stars in the sky

That gave light to the darkness

FEARLESS/CARE-LESS

One day at school

Sitting under the tree

A classmate asks for a quarter

I had no silvers

Only dollar bills

He said give me the dollar

I said no

He sat on the side of me

Pull out a knife

I told him calmly

If you are going to stab me

Then stab me

But you are not getting my dollar

I do not know what I was thinking

But I was not afraid

He left

And my dollar was still in my pocket

It is hard to understand

But when you grow up poor

Having done without

A dollar is a lot

FINDING MY GIFT

In grade 11

My best friend, Lawrence

Said to me

Let us join this reading competition

It was a competition

Held by the school

Where students borrow books from the library

Read it and then write a report about it

The goal was who can read the most books

In a certain period of time

I was reluctant

But if Lawrence was doing it

Then I was doing it

I entered

And I won

It was here that I fell in love with reading

My aunt had a collection of books at home

I would read them all

They would take me away

I would go on the most amazing adventures

My favorite book

The Pillars of the Earth

That was a book

That opened my imagination

Grade 12 came along

And the competition came again

I had to defend my crown

There was always a poetry competition

I had never written poetry before

But I entered

I won the reading competition again

And place in the top 7 for the poetry

I was proud of myself

But more importantly

I had found my gift

I wrote pages and pages of poetry

I finally found a way

To let everything out

Although sometimes I would write

And never wanted to see certain poems again

There were just too sad

I let them out

But I did not let them go

Progress

SCHOOL

School was a roller coaster

It hard to be successful without money

But not impossible

From days of getting free lunch

In primary school

To days with no lunch

In Senior school

My aunt Wendy

Always tells me

She does not know

How I made it

Only God

And sheer will power

In Senior high

I took up Agriculture and Food and Nutrition

Many days I had no money

To buy supplies

To cook in school

So, I stayed home

I did not want to be asked

Why I don't have any supplies

I always pass that class though

But I was never near

My full potential

I wanted to be a prefect

But I had no passport size pictures

I had no photos at all

To apply

I remember the lady asking

When I went for the form

Are you sure you have a 2.0 average

People can be judgmental

I remember Literature class

I did not have

The textbook for the class

The teacher

Ms. Rolle

Put everyone out the class

Who had no textbook

Punish for being poor

My term grade was an F

But I got the highest on the exam

An A

I pass the class with a C+

One-point shy of a B-

I told you

I was resilient

NO ONE KNOWS

As a teenage male

Who do you tell?

That you are in pain

That is not physical

No father

No mother

Everyone is on fire

You are trying to rescue them

You are so numb

You do not realize

You are on fire too

No one knows

That I hate being alone so much

That I constantly eat

To distract my mind

From the emptiness

No, I was not weak

I did not want to be a victim

To cut myself

To smoke

To join some gang

Searching for love

I could not get at home

But in the end

I was a victim

None the less

Just a different version

COMING BACK

I had a government summer job

Making $100 a week

Which is a lot for me

We got paid in a lump sum

After six weeks

I got a check for $600

I spent about 30 to cash it

My mother came back to "visit."

And she took every last cent

I gave it to her

And she took it

She did not bring anything

But she left full

Silly of me

Trying to buy love

It always leaves you

Broken

When was someone

Going to care for me

NUMB

Sitting in my religious studies class

Taking to two classmates

I had mention

Something about my parents

One of the young lady's replied

I thought your parents were dead

You never mention them

I was always

A bit

Calm

Numb

Emotionless

I remember

My uncle being

In a drug fuel rage

Shirtless with a machete

Wanting to attack his brother girlfriend

Who was quite pregnant

She refuses to go inside

To the safety of the house

So am standing in between them

A crowd gathering in the road

Watching

My uncle would charge

Then back off

Am thinking

I will have to be a hero today

Dead is subject too

Interpretation

NOT OKAY

INTERLUDE

I graduated High School

Won a few awards

I was set free

Whatever free is

It was great to win something

But when you have worked

Three years for it

It was great to earn something

Graduated with

Agriculture and Religious Studies award

Validation I guess

That the years

We're not wasted

I had survived

That jungle

But I now I have

A bigger one

It took me quite a while

To find a steady job

It is like everybody expected me

To figure it out on my own

I remember my aunt telling me

I had a few weeks to find a job

Or I would get kicked out

My family is unrelenting

Unapologetic

In their ignorance

Not all of them

But the majority

They want the benefits you can bring

But not the broken pieces

Being an adult

Does not make the pain go away

It just makes broken pieces

Sharper

MISSING CHILD

I miss never being a child

I miss never having toys

I regret the pain of family

Of having to swallow my emotions

And be as cold

As a December night sky

Sometimes I wonder what I could be

If I was not such a machine

I miss my father

Who I never got to call dad

Because he did not care enough

To be in my life

Being an adult is hard enough

But being an adult as a child

That is like five years of therapy

But I guess am okay

TRIGGER

Am afraid at times

That my mind

Like a power circuit

Will overload

And the pain

I held at bay all my life

Will finally be free

Like that scared child

Playing alone in the dark

It is best not to feel sorry for me

Am better alone

It is safer

But am the sweetest person ever

But like Carrie at the prom

Sometimes the quietness

Hides something so terrifying

Pain can trigger anything

BEHIND THE MASK

I love it when it rains

When it rains

I can smile

Because the tears cannot be seen

Hidden

Like water under the sea

I hate the sun

So bright

It stares at you

Like a billion eyes

Forcing you to smile

Harden the mask

Because I do not need

These tears to be seen

CAN I DREAM?

We push people to work

But never to dream

To make money

But not goals

I have learned

That work is not the answer

Just another journey

It is a good distraction

But no amount of money

Can make you happy

You can cover the hurt

Dress it in 24 karat gold

Post it on Instagram

But the damage is still there

The first few years of work

My mother benefited the most

Although she was overseas

Every time she needed something

She would call me

Which was like twice a month

The only times I would hear from her

I gave, and I gave

Because that is what good kids do?

Parents wonder why

Children leave home

And go someplace far away

To never return

I never got

Christmas gifts

Birthday gifts

The only time

My parents remembered me

Is when they needed me

They were a job all by themselves

TOO GOOD

Up to this point

Never had my own bed

All my life

It has been

Couches and floors

Never had a room to call my own

So, to me

Bed was a luxury

Something most people

Do not think about

I remember going into the bathroom

To getaway

Locking the door

Sitting in the tub

With my clothes on

So that I could take a nap in peace

A bathroom

That was new

Grew up with outside toilet and iron tubs

Then my aunt moved away

Got her own house

And I got her room

Took twenty years

But progress is progress

Paid my uncle

To fix the wooden floors

Went and brought

A brand-new bed

Finally

My own bed and room

Few months later

Christmas Time

Always loved

Christmas Time

It is the one time

Everyone was happy

I brought decoration for my room

Had a table

With bowls

Fill with walnuts. kisses and candy

It was happiness and peace

Then

My mother came

To visit

I could not let her sleep on the couch

So, I gave her the bed and the room

Back to the couch, I go

Tired

GRANDFATHER

My Grandfather

Is the closest thing

I have ever saw

To what God

Wanted Adam to be

Of my entire family

I was most like him

He was the kindest person

What he had

He shared with his family

But he was unapologetic with his words

Not rude

But direct and blunt

The type that catches people off-guard

In a society of cyberbullying and gossiping

For my entire life

I remember my Grandfather as being blind

My Grandfather came from a time

Where only the rich had cars

And everyone else walked miles and miles

He only went as far as Grade 6

But somehow

Smarter than most people I know

He had a farm at one point

That went neglected by his children

I would have loved to have seen it

One of the awards I graduated with

Was agriculture

So, I love growing things

I had to watch him

Be bedridden

By cancer

In his 80's

He still had his own teeth

Meat on his bones

He was fit as a horse

But cancer had deflated him

In the same room

His wife

My Grandmother died in

I went to work one day

And came home

To hear he was in the hospital

He died that day

They both were gone

There was nothing left

Keeping the fragile bones

Of this family together

GOD CAN DREAM A BIGGER DREAM

I never thought

I could afford college

It seemed a luxury

That was beyond me

I wanted to go

But my paycheck was only entry level

But it was being at work that pushed me

The way I saw power was abuse

And given as a reward for loyalty

I did not want to be a victim

To be the guy at the bottom who complained

So, I got a loan and went to college

My first semester

I remembered Phycology class

We had to write our goals

I wrote that

I wanted a 4.0 G.P. A

And to graduated valedictorian

The Professor collected it

And returned it with a smiley face

I was there for a year

The work was fine

But the financial burden was overwhelming

There were days I was hungry

With no money

I was paying back a loan

While working fewer days to attend school

It was too much

With so little

But it was a successful year

But those goals did not come to past

Everything happens for a reason

I have learned that

RAINING

No one understands

The feeling of emptiness

The feeling of

Knowing the little money, you have

Probably will not last the week

Thinking to yourself

How will I eat

Suddenly McDonald's seems a luxury

It is like you are in a hole

Made of sand

And it is raining

And you are trying to get out

No one understands

That poverty is more potent than any bullet

For too died is to escape

And am here

Family looking for me for help

And the walls I have in my mind

I must turn into armor

In real life to fight

JESUS

Lately

My mind has been overwhelmed

Not like water in the ocean

But like water in the desert

Am not enough to quench the thirst

Of the world around me

To many eyes

To many mirrors

All were wanting my attention

So, I stopped

Like a lion

When its prey spots it

In that second

Everybody thinks

What do I do?

So today

I let the phone rang until it stops

Today was Sunday

But I could be nobody Jesus

And today

My mind said thank you

Best day in a while

POND

When I switch college

I remember

Mr. Sands

One of my teachers

Saying that this was a pond

I thought to myself

What a perfect description

When I graduated with my Associate Degree

I remember feeling

Disappointed I did not get valedictorian

I found out later

That only those graduating with Bachelors

Are considered for valedictorian

When it was my time to graduated with my B.A,

I paid the graduation fee

And then I decided I would not attend

I didn't see the point in going

I could always pick up my degree later

I didn't even tell anyone I was graduating

Then one evening I got a call

It was from my school

I was valedictorian

And had to give a speech

I was stunned

Unbelievable

Was this my color purple moment

The dream had come true

Tears in my eyes

The dream had come true

I gave the speech of my life

I had defied the odds

And written my own story

A month later

I was promoted to management at work

I often think back

On that little boy

Who made the decision

To be different

LOVE YOURSELF

I found love

It was magic

Fell in love

On the first day

It was not rush

It seemed to be destiny

Finally, after an eternity of winter

There was the warmth of love

It was beautiful

I love them with all of me

 Broken pieces and all

I showed my scars and said

Here I Am

I even cried

Which is a lot for me

Two things I do not like to do in front of people

Sleep and cried

Do not like being that vulnerable

But I was

To find out

That I was pouring into a cracked vessel

You never practice lying

Just withholding the truth

It slowly cracked under the pressure

Of true love

For me

It was a valuable lesson

For although I love you

I had to love myself enough

To let you go

Perhaps the hardest decision

I have ever made

HATE

People will hate you

Just because

God bless you

I have encounter

Many fragile men

With positions and ego

Like Joseph with his brothers

I did nothing wrong

Sometimes people see your potential

When you are just simply

Trying to be

But who God bless

No man can hurt

The wait on God

Is worth it

When I start my job

As an on caller

A few months in

My manager told me

I would be taken

Off the schedule

For slow season was approaching

I told him

God would make a way

Instead of being removed

I was made permanent

He probably wanted to see my reaction

But I have always known

No one is entitled to anything

No matter how amazing they are

I have had power

Before I had a title

Had influence

Before I had power

I have been in the pit

And praise my way through

SINK IN

Some humans are like vampires

You let them suck you dry

Hoping you can please them

But when you are empty

They go away

They change

And you sit here

Hurt

Confused

Anger building

Like a spark in a forest

Here we are again

You cannot change anybody

When will it sink in

GOD AND I

God is always here

He is only waiting for us

To acknowledge him

To stop trying to do it on our own

That every pain

Every struggle

Was only a test

A journey necessary

It is my faith in God

That has sustained me

On this journey

For he gives us

What we need

And not what we want

Every decision made now

Shapes the future

Never wanted to be a victim

Attention magnify things

We must be careful

What we focus on

I AM OKAY

I am fine

A program response

From the mask I wear

Because I cannot let them in

Am Fine

I say with a smile

That a diamond would envy

As they look into my eyes

To see into my soul

But am no amateur

Even my eyes shine

Like the sea

On a hot summer day

But then something happened

An accident at work

As I laid on a hospital bed

The doctor asks, "how are you."

And I said

Am fine

And he replied

"Then why are you here."

I thought to myself

I had a 6ft

150lbs

Metal Box

Fall on my neck

Had to be lifted

From the floor to

The ambulance bed

Neck place in a neck brace

And the automated response is

I am fine

How much hurt

Do you have to go through

To be that numb

And the mask cracked

The walls collapse

As my brain and heart

Scramble to readjust

I realize what I always knew

That it is okay

Not to be okay.

It is okay to cry

To let it out

So, let us talk about it

And together we will be okay

PROGRESS

The things that plague me

Mentally in my youth

Now seems like a speck of dust

On a mountain top

Insignificant

Unworthy of my time

There comes in a time in a person life

When you just do not care

As you get older

The roller coaster

Is no longer up and down

Its more smooth

With a dip here and there

This is the time

That people think you have changed

But by the grace of God

I have not just simply changed

I have grown

And growing up

Never felt so good

HOMETOWN

I went back to the village

Yesterday

With nothing to prove

And nothing to show

Except for the smile on my face

I saw a man who I had known for many years

We caught up on old times

As I was leaving

He said

"He was proud of me."

Something in my mind shattered

It was like the sound of thunder

Over the desert plain

And for once I embrace the rain

Someone was proud of me

I waited 28 years to hear that

I wanted to shed a tear

Those words were as powerful

As I love you

Perhaps even more powerful

Because they were real

And wanted nothing in return

"He was proud of me."

At this point in my life

I had done okay

I had gotten that 4.0

Earned that Valedictorian

Work my way into management

But to me

It only scratches the surface of my potential

In the words of Ms. Winfrey

Every person wants to know

Do you see me?

Do you hear me?

Do I matter?

For once

Somebody said yes

Thank You

I never wrote to rhyme

I wrote to bleed

To tell the story of me

To drain this poison

That penetrated this seed

I did not want to die

Pretending to be okay

Like the absence of my father

The color of my skin

And the poverty it came with

Did not make me cry

When I was alone

In my head

Surrounded by family

How can one drown on land?

When the pain never ends

Thank you for allowing me to bleed

To breathe

To be me

A human

A man

Black

Fatherless

Motherless

But not lost

To be Continued

Conclusion

I mourn you

Too young

Too kind

Why did you try being there for everybody

Only to lose yourself

Why did you try being their sun

Just to get lost in the darkness

I mourn you

Your emptiness

The love you always wanted

But never received

The pain you kept locked away

Because you thought

Yourself unworthy

Of happiness

Of love

I mourn the boy

Who never got his father

The boy who walks around

With a force field around him

Letting no one in

I mourn you out loud

Am sorry

I want you to know

That I did my best

Surround by

Drugs, poverty, and violence

I wanted you to be different

Like Moses in a basket

I hid within myself

It is easy to wonder

How things could have been

Too many ifs

Forgive me

For all the times

I did not rise to the occasion

For all the times

I have been scared

To speak

To be great

Still stuck in my mind

Stuck in my pain

But I let you go

I let you go

So, I can be

The man you can be proud of

Say Something.

Printed in Great Britain
by Amazon

80033346R00061